For Michele Burgess & Bill Kelly,
who follow their own path
—M.B.

THIS IS A BORZOI BOOK PUBLISHED BY ALFRED A. KNOPF

Text copyright © 2024 by Matthew Burgess
Jacket art and interior illustrations copyright © 2024 by Marc Majewski

All rights reserved. Published in the United States by Alfred A. Knopf,
an imprint of Random House Children's Books,
a division of Penguin Random House LLC, New York.

Knopf, Borzoi Books, and the colophon are
registered trademarks of Penguin Random House LLC.

Visit us on the Web! rhcbooks.com

Educators and librarians, for a variety of teaching tools,
visit us at RHTeachersLibrarians.com

Library of Congress Cataloging-in-Publication Data is available upon request.
ISBN 978-1-9848-9380-2 (trade) — ISBN 978-1-9848-9381-9 (lib. bdg.) —
ISBN 978-1-9848-9382-6 (ebook)

The text of this book is set in 16-point Griffo Classico.
The illustrations were created using acrylics on paper.

Editor: Esther Cajahuaringa
Designer: Nicole de las Heras
Copy Editor: Artie Bennett
Managing Editor: Jake Eldred
Production Manager: Claribel Vasquez

MANUFACTURED IN CHINA
10 9 8 7 6 5 4 3 2 1
First Edition

AS EDWARD IMAGINED

A Story of Edward Gorey in Three Acts

Words by
Matthew Burgess

Pictures by
Marc Majewski

Alfred A. Knopf
New York

Edward St. John Gorey peeked from the window
of his grandparents' house as train cars clacked
and rattled across the railroad tracks.

Amazed, he picked up a pencil and made
his very first drawing, "The Sausage Train,"
which his mother treasured and saved.

At three and a half, Edward
taught himself how to read.

His father gave him permission
to prowl his personal library,

and Edward stalked the shelves
like an inquisitive cat,
pawing this and reading that.

He followed Alice
down
the
rabbit
hole
into Wonderland.

Wowed by the detailed drawings
in *Winnie-the-Pooh*, he lost himself
in the Hundred Acre Wood.

And before he turned six, he finished a long,
spooky novel about a vampire named . . .

DRACULA.

"MUA-HA-HA-HA!"

Soon Edward began conjuring his own spine-tingling stories.

He crafted a book titled "Hand of Doom," in which
a skeleton's fingers crept
from page
to page.

Even from a young age, Edward had a flair
for doing things his own delightfully peculiar way,
like painting his toenails green and strutting
down a fancy street in bare feet—

daring to live the life he imagined.

ACT TWO
Edward in
the City

After graduating from college, Edward moved
from Boston to the bustling island of Manhattan.

People took note of the tall, bearded man
in a long fur coat with tennis shoes
and plenty of clinking rings.

"I just can't go out of the house with naked fingers."

And where was he going?

To the New York City Ballet!

Entranced by the dancers and the choreography,
Edward attended nearly every performance for over
twenty years—even the Saturday matinees.

Edward had found a job illustrating the covers of others' books,
but at home, surrounded by his cats, he wrote and drew
his own story about a mustachioed novelist named Mr. Earbrass.

This first book didn't make a big splash.

Neither did his second, nor his third, nor his fourth.

But Edward kept creating. . . .

And with each book, more and more readers discovered his stylish drawings, his outlandish poetry, and his deliciously sinister sense of humor.

Edward imagined alligators riding bicycles,

cats
dancing
ballet,

and a grinning monster
called a Wuggly Ump
chasing singing children.

Edward's following grew and grew, and one day,
he was invited to design the costumes and the sets for a play
about a vampire named . . .

DRACULA.
"MUA-HA-HA-HA!"

Dracula was a smash on Broadway
and Edward was nominated for important awards.

But he dreaded the thought of walking the red carpet
with all the posing and the preening and the paparazzi.

"I began to realize what it would be like to be rich and famous, but I've decided unh-unh."

So instead, he watched at home with his cats.

ACT THREE
At Home
by the Sea

At the height of his success,
Edward decided to leave the city
and move to a small town by the sea.

When the ballet closed for the season,
he packed the car, took his cats,
and drove to Cape Cod, Massachusetts.

Edward lived at 8 Strawberry Lane,
in a place he called Elephant House.

Formerly owned by a sea captain,
it was a squeaky, creaky, leaky fixer-upper,
but Edward made it home.

Here, he could write and draw in peace,
and, of course, enjoy his six cats' acrobatics.

Edward didn't mind when they left paw prints behind,
but if they knocked bottles of ink across his drawings,
he would insist:

"Snuggy-poos, desist!"

With plenty of space to himself,
Edward's collections grew:

teddy bears, sea stones,
skeletons of all sizes and shapes,
and books by the thousands!

Now he could prowl his personal library

like a lanky, bespectacled cat,
pawing this and reading that.

Edward continued to make many new books.

He also worked with actors in local theaters,
creating original plays with titles like:

*Crazed Teacups, Stuffed Elephants,
Lost Shoelaces, Flapping Ankles,*
and *Heads Will Roll.*

Edward was content to do his own thing,
in his own way, in his own time.

He lived his life precisely as he wished—
and when, one day, he passed away, the cats wondered
where their dear Edward had gone.

They missed him, of course,
as did his family, friends, and fans.

But in the many books Edward left behind . . .

Mr. Earbrass still broods and frets,

the alligator rides the bicycle on his back,

and from deep inside the Wuggly Ump,

the children sing glogalimp, glugalump,

just as

Edward imagined.

Author's Note

Once you cross the threshold into Edward Gorey's world, you never forget the experience. His drawing and his writing are so singular, so wonderfully particular to his imagination, that his books often defy classification. Yet Gorey is widely recognized as a major American artist of the twentieth century, and you can see his influence in the work of many contemporary artists and storytellers.

When I found Edward Gorey's books as a kid, I was charmed and challenged simultaneously. The spooky elements surprised me, the drawings drew me in, and everything seemed suffused with a gleefully unserious wink. Reading these books felt like a real discovery—there was nothing else like them—and for a long time the identity of the author remained an intriguing mystery.

The more I learned about Edward as a person, the more I liked him. From early childhood to the very end, he was intensely creative, and in both art and life, he was completely himself. This is one of the reasons I want to share his story with young readers. I remember, as a child, how important it was to encounter grown-ups who followed their own path. We all need people to remind us that we can be truly ourselves, and that we are free to create and even inhabit the worlds we imagine.

And yes, in Edward's case, a world filled with cats! He lived with up to six at one time, but that was his limit. "Seven cats is too many cats," he would say. In fact, he became such a stalwart advocate for all animals that he left the bulk of his estate to a charitable trust supporting cats, dogs, and other species, including bats and elephants. He even stopped wearing his iconic fur coats for this reason.

With this book we hope to offer a portrait of Edward as a person and not a caricature. He wasn't quite the gloomy recluse that some imagine; he was brilliant, funny, eccentric, and a good friend. The owner of Jack's Outback, the Cape Cod diner where Edward ate every day for over a decade, described him with the warmest words: "He was a joy." Following his own delightfully peculiar path, the boy who read *Dracula* cover to cover grew up to design a Broadway play bearing his name, and when fame came calling, he chose creative freedom above all. So fitting, so Edward.

—Matthew Burgess

More About Edward

Dery, Mark. *Born to Be Posthumous: The Eccentric Life and Mysterious Genius of Edward Gorey.* New York: Little, Brown and Company, 2018.

Gorey, Edward. *Ascending Peculiarity: Edward Gorey on Edward Gorey.* Interviews selected and edited by Karen Wilkin. New York: Harcourt, Inc., 2001.

The Edward Gorey Charitable Trust. edwardgorey.org

The Edward Gorey House. edwardgoreyhouse.org

Quotation Sources & Citations

"I just can't go out of the house with naked fingers." *Ascending Peculiarity: Edward Gorey on Edward Gorey.* Interviews selected and edited by Karen Wilkin.

"I began to realize what it would be like to be rich and famous, but I've decided unh-unh." Mark Dery, *Born to Be Posthumous: The Eccentric Life and Mysterious Genius of Edward Gorey.*

"Snuggy-poos, desist!" Alexander Theroux, *The Strange Case of Edward Gorey.*

Tim Gray

Edward Gorey at home in Cape Cod with one of his cats.

Chronology

1925	Edward is born on February 22 in Chicago, Illinois.
1926–28	He makes his first drawing at eighteen months old and teaches himself to read at three and a half.
1931	At age six, Edward skips first grade and enrolls in second at a nearby Catholic school.
1937	Following his parents' divorce, Edward moves with his mother to Miami, Florida. He keeps a baby alligator as a pet. In his diary, he writes about his love of cats.
1938–42	With his mother, Edward returns to Chicago and enrolls at Francis W. Parker School. The arts are central to the school's curriculum, and here Edward's sense of himself as an artist takes shape.
1942	Edward graduates from high school at seventeen years old. He is awarded a scholarship to Harvard, but with the draft looming, he postpones his acceptance and attends the Art Institute of Chicago for the fall term.
1944	Edward is drafted into the U.S. Army. For two years, he serves as a clerk at Dugway Proving Ground in Utah.
1946	After the war, Edward enrolls at Harvard, majoring in French literature. The poet Frank O'Hara is his roommate. He continues writing, drawing, and developing as an artist.
1953	Edward is offered a position illustrating books at Doubleday Anchor in New York City.
	Edward publishes his first book, *The Unstrung Harp*. He begins making regular visits to the Gotham Book Mart and becomes close friends with the bookshop's founder, Frances Steloff. He will exhibit his artwork here for the rest of his life.
1962	Edward creates his own imprint, the Fantod Press, which allows him to publish whatever he wishes. Sometimes he uses anagrammatic pen names, such as Ogdred Weary, Garrod Weedy, Mrs. Regera Dowdy, and Raddory Gewe.

1972	He publishes his first anthology, titled *Amphigorey,* containing fifteen of his early works. Three more anthologies follow: *Amphigorey Too* (1975), *Amphigorey Also* (1983), and *Amphigorey Again* (2006).
1973–77	Edward designs a production of *Dracula* for a small theater on Nantucket. Years later, in 1977, the play opens as *Edward Gorey's Dracula* on Broadway. He wins a Tony Award for Best Costume Design.
1979	Edward uses his royalties from *Dracula* to purchase the two-hundred-year-old home of a sea captain on the Yarmouth Port Common, on Cape Cod.
1980	Gorey is invited to design animated introductions for PBS's *Mystery!* series. They become some of his most iconic work.
1983	When the revered choreographer for the New York City Ballet George Balanchine passes away on April 30, 1983, Edward decides to move to Cape Cod.
1986	After working on renovations to his house in Yarmouth Port for seven years, Edward finally moves in for good. He continues to make new books and stage original plays with actors in local theaters throughout Cape Cod.
2000	Edward dies of a heart attack at age seventy-five on April 15, 2000. After his death, his home is converted into the Edward Gorey House, a landmark and museum that hosts annual exhibitions, literary programs, and children's events.

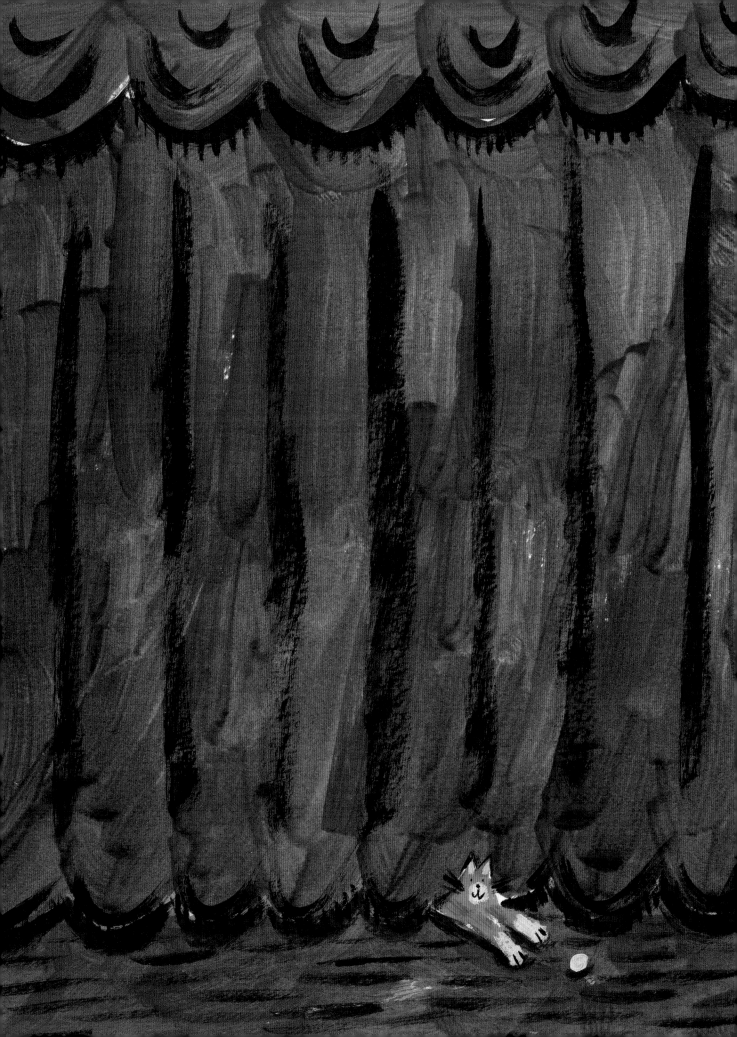